For Systa, who marched downtown on October 24, 1975, and did not cook or clean or watch the children,
but instead sang, chanted, and was so inspired that she remembers the day as if it were yesterday.

—L.Ó.

**"Step up girl, be unshy. Let your blanket fly. Over fields and over space,
all the world observe in pace."**❋

—Bríet Bjarnhéðinsdóttir* (1856–1940)

❋Quote translation by Halla Kjartansdóttir
*Bríet Bjarnhéðinsdóttir was an early Icelandic advocate for women's liberation
and a fighter for women's right to vote. She sewed these words on a blanket for her daughter,
Laufey, as an encouragement for her to steer her own ship (or her own magic blanket),
to be her own boss, and to not let anything stop her.

Photographs on pages 36–37 courtesy of the Reykjavik Museum of Photography

Book design by Melissa Nelson Greenberg
Design assistance by Shriya Jayanthi

Library of Congress Cataloging-in-Publication Data available.
ISBN: 978-1-951836-90-0

Printed in China

10 9 8 7 6 5 4 3 2 1

CAMERON KIDS is an imprint of CAMERON + COMPANY

CAMERON + COMPANY
Petaluma, California
www.cameronbooks.com

Special thanks to Gerður Steinþórsdóttir, Sigríður Lillý Baldursdóttir, Sumargjöf Children's Association, and the Iceland Literature Center.

LINDA ÓLAFSDÓTTIR

I DARE!

I CAN!

I WILL!

THE DAY THE ICELANDIC WOMEN WALKED OUT AND INSPIRED THE WORLD

 cameron kids

Vera watched as her mamma put on a bright red beret.
"Today is going to be a special day," Mamma said, tying a yellow scarf on Vera.

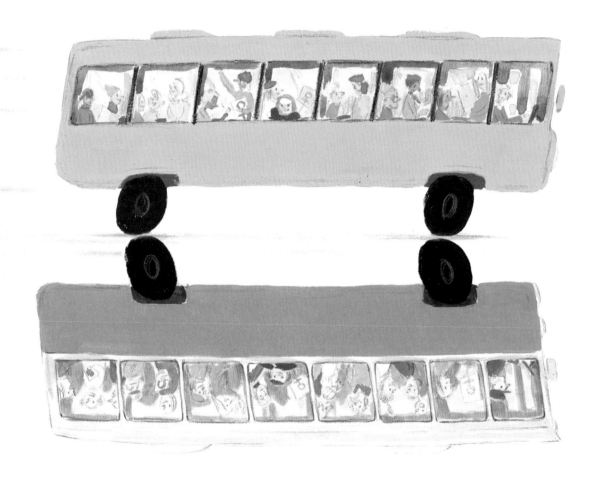

"On this day, when I was your age, I marched downtown with my mamma and thousands of women. It was the Women's Day Off, or the Long Friday, as some called it."

"IT'S FRIDAY, OCTOBER, 24, 1975, AND CROWDS ARE EXPECTED TO GATHER IN DOWNTOWN REYKJAVÍK AND THROUGHOUT THE COUNTRY AS THE WOMEN OF ICELAND WALK OUT..."

"Was it longer than other days?" Vera asked.

Mamma laughed, "Well, maybe not in hours, but many thought the day would never end, especially my dad.

"Because on October 24th, 1975, women all over Iceland
marched out of their homes and jobs. They took the day off."

"They did? Why?"

"For a long time, before I was born, women had been fighting for equal rights. It used to be that boys were sent to school, but girls were kept home to learn how to take care of the household and the children."

"Mamma, that is *ridiculous*!"

"The very few girls who were allowed an education were still encouraged to get married and become housewives after graduation."

"Slowly, more women got educations and started working outside the home. They became teachers, doctors, and nurses and found work in the banks and the fish factories.

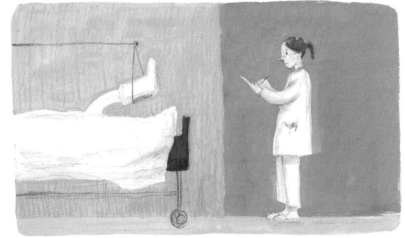

"But they got only about half the pay the men got. And they did all this while caring for their families as well.

"And every day they were treated poorly. They had to pay to use the public restroom.

"They didn't have their names in the phone book, on the doorbell, or on the mail.

"They felt invisible."

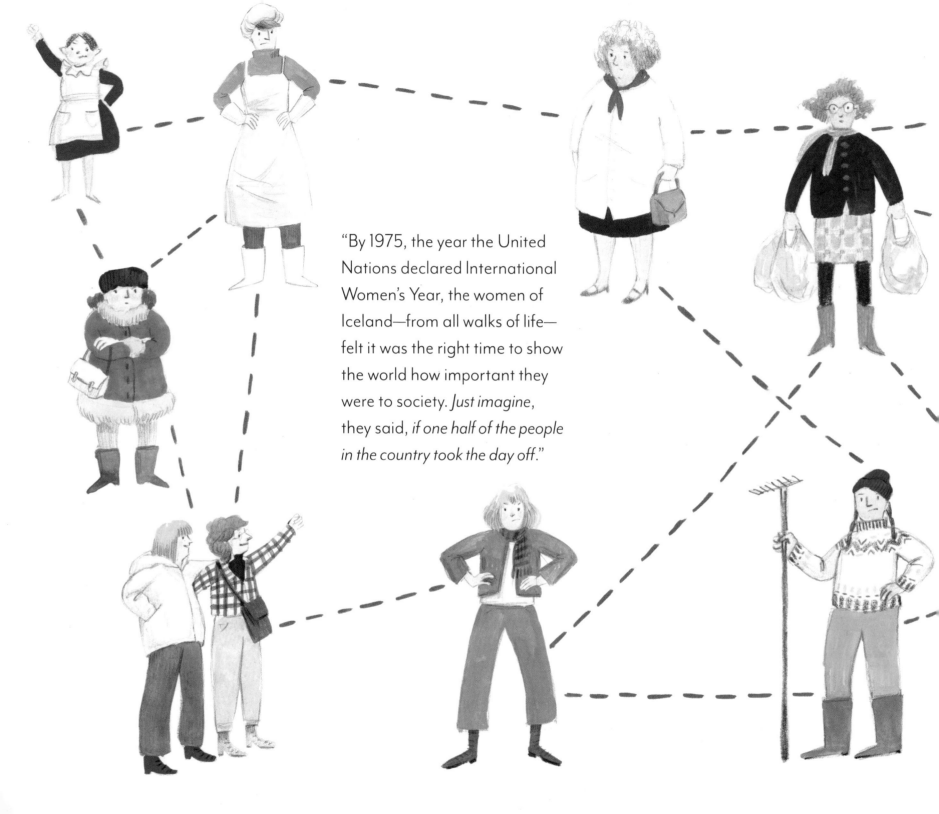

"By 1975, the year the United Nations declared International Women's Year, the women of Iceland—from all walks of life—felt it was the right time to show the world how important they were to society. *Just imagine,* they said, *if one half of the people in the country took the day off.*"

"And they came. At exactly 2:00 p.m., the women of Iceland walked out of their jobs and homes. They did not cook or clean or watch the children, but instead sang and cheered.

"When I walked out of the bus, I joined a stream of women from every direction, gathering in a sea of more people than I knew even existed!"

"Ninety percent of women all over the country went on a strike."

"When the women walked out, the men had to do the women's jobs—all of them.

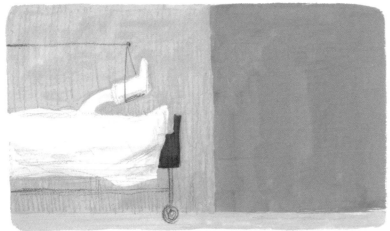

"And take care of the children. Just like the women did every single day."

"It was not just in the city of Reykjavík where the women walked out; it was all over the country—

"Women farmworkers marched through small towns.

"Women working at the butchers started a water fight with their boss when he objected to them joining the march—

"Women on a fishing boat stayed in their bunkers and convinced the captain to send a telegram to the march in Reykjavík, where it was read out loud to the roaring cheer of the crowd."

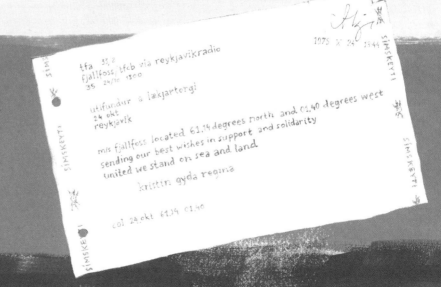

"And the city was packed!"

"Everyone sang and cheered,

I DARE!
I CAN!
I WILL!

"It was truly a special day."

"On the way home, I felt so lucky to have been a part of the Women's Day Off. My father greeted us like never before.

"And he made us dinner for the first time.

"'That felt like the longest day,' he said. 'How was it?'

"We told him all about it over soup."

"The news of the women who took the day off in Iceland spread around the world. Calls, telegrams, and letters were sent: 'How did you do it?' 'How can *we* do it?'

"In the years to come, there were women's strikes all over the word, inspired by the Icelandic women.

"Women's rights have no borders."

IGUALDAD AHORA
EQUALITY
THE TIME IS NOW
STRAJK KOBIET!
OUT OF THE KITCHENS AND INTO THE WORLD
वशि्व की महहलिाएं एक हों
libertad

"Today, we must continue to fight for what we believe in and demand equal rights for everyone.

"We must remember the women who came before us, who dared that they could.

"Will you dare?" asked Mamma.

Vera shouted, "I WILL!"

But, dare I, can I, will I?

Yes, I dare, I can, I will!

And later the children will say:

Thank you, mothers, you sure cleaned it up.

Yes, later the children will say,

Because this is the exact world that I want.

But, dare I, can I, will I?

Yes, I dare, I can, I will!

—From a verse of the Swedish battle song, translated in English to "Go Girls!" and known in Iceland as "Áfram stelpur!"

October 24, 1975, the Women's Day Off at Lækjartorg; Guðrún Erlendsdóttir, the director of the Women's Day Off. Photo credit: Björgvin Pálsson

The day the Icelandic women walked out and inspired the world happened in the year of 1975—declared International Women's Year by the United Nations. The theme was "Equality, Development, and Peace," as the UN wanted to draw worldwide attention to full gender equality.

Unions, governments, and women's organizations in countries all over the world prepared for International Women's Year and the UN Conference held in Mexico City that summer. In the aftermath of the conference, women in Iceland felt that this was the time to take action at home. They wanted to draw attention to the unsung contributions of women to Icelandic society—and the fact that women were paid only a fraction of what men received for the same amount of work.

Drawing from the ideas dreamed up by women worldwide, they realized that the best way to show their impact, worth, and value in society was for the women of Iceland to take the day off and let their absence speak for itself. Women's organizations formed groups to organize their strike and spread the word.

They chose October 24—United Nations Day.

Their goal was to gather women from all walks of life—housewives, office workers, farmers, teachers, bakers, senior citizens, and students, alike—and throughout the country, from the city of Reykjavík to the smallest towns. These thousands of women and girls were all different and unique, but they all had something very much in common—they were undervalued by society, and they were determined for that to change.

On that Long Friday, the women who marched downtown to the stage at Lækjartorg Square in Reykjavík couldn't believe their eyes. It was packed—not just in the city but in small towns across the country! More than 25,000 women gathered in Reykjavík alone, which was an astonishing number, considering that Iceland's population at the

October 24, 1975, the Women's Day Off. From Menntaskólinn við Tjörnina (high school) in Reykjavík. Male teachers take care of the staff members' children, trying to fill in after most of the women in the city walked out of their jobs in protest. Photo credit: Ari Kárason (1919–1997)

time was just under 220,000 people. It is believed that 90 percent of women from all over Iceland participated. And on this historic day, they demanded equality—equal pay for equal work, equal opportunities for education and employment, the right over their own bodies, and to be valued the same as men.

The Women's Day Off was heard all over the world! It helped realize long-held dreams: In 1980, Vigdís Finnbogadóttir became the first woman—not only in Iceland, but in the world—to be democratically elected as a president. After the historic election, women's political parties were founded, and women's rights became an important issue on the political agenda in Iceland. In the years to come, day care and preschools were improved, as well as maternity and paternity leave.

Today, Iceland is one of the most gender-equal countries in the world. But even now, the pay gap between men and women still persists—the average income of women is about 77 percent of the average income of men. And so, women march on. The Women's Day Off was held again in 1985, 2005, 2010, 2016, and 2018, and it has inspired marches in many countries. Although the struggle for women's rights has come a long way, it is still important to march and fight, because women all over the world are still being denied equality.

By remembering the people who fought for human rights worldwide, we understand the power of unity and the importance of continuing to fight for what we believe in.

WE DARE! WE CAN! WE WILL!

October 24, 1975, the Women's Day Off. A group of women on the stage on Lækjartorg (from left: Bríet Héðinsdóttir, Elísabet Gunnarsdóttir, Steinunn Jóhannesdóttir, Margrét Helga Jóhannsdóttir, Kristín Jónsdóttir, Halla Guðmundsdóttir, unknown, Þuríður Magnúsdóttir. Lækjartorg, Reykjavík). Photo credit: Bjarnleifur Bjarnleifsson (1915–1987)